W9-DEV-681

This book belongs to:
_____

Published by Penguin Books India
11 Community Centre, Panchsheel Park, New Delhi 110017

1   3 5 7 9 10 8 6 4 2

Printed at Ajanta Offset & Packagings Ltd, New Delhi

Food

illustrated by R.C. Prakash

We eat food all day round.
Food gives us energy.

We get a lot of food
from plants.
People grow plants in
farms and gardens.

This is how we get food from plants.

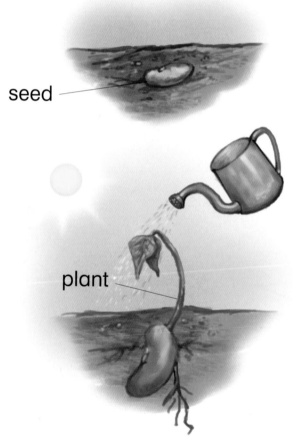

seed

plant

leaf

fruit

Sometimes we eat the plant's fruit.

bell pepper

tomato

ladies' fingers

beans

eggplant

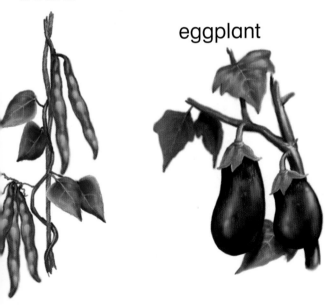

13

Sometimes we eat the plant's leaves.

spinach

cabbage

lettuce

Sometimes we eat the plant's roots.

potato

carrot

radish

17

Sometimes we eat the plant's seeds.

wheat

kidney beans

chickpeas

Sometimes we eat fruit we get from trees.

jackfruit

mango

Sometimes we eat food we get from animals.

milk

eggs

meat

fish

23

We eat different types of
food to grow strong.

beans

fruits

vegetables

dairy products

Sometimes we eat raw food.
Sometimes we cook
the food.

27

Choose your favourite food!

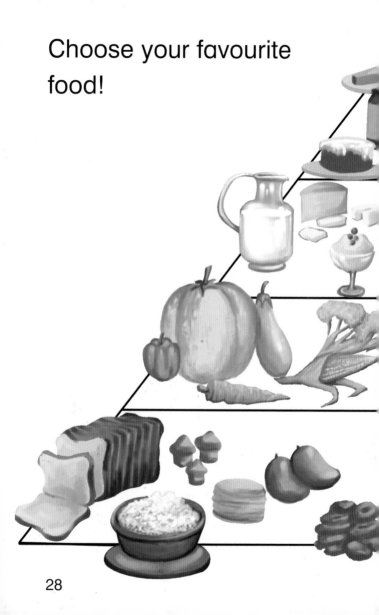

Index